Texas History

Mary Dodson Wade

Heinemann Library
Chicago, Illinois

© 2004, 2008 Heinemann Library
an imprint of Capstone Global Library, LLC.
Chicago, Illinois

Customer Service 888-454-2279

Visit our website at **www.heinemannlibrary.com**

All rights reserved. No part of this publication may be reproduced or transmitted in any form or by any means, electronic or mechanical, including photocopying, recording, taping, or any information storage and retrieval system, without permission in writing from the publisher.

Designed by Kimberly R. Miracle and Betsy Wernert
Photo Research by Tracy Cummins
Printed and bound in the united States of America, North Mankato, MN

13 12 11
10 9 8 7 6 5 4 3 2

New edition ISBNs: 978-1-4329-1151-5 (hardcover)
978-1-4329-1158-4 (paperback)

The Library of Congress has cataloged the first edition as follows:
Wade, Mary Dodson.
 Texas history / Mary Dodson Wade.
  v. cm. -- (Heinemann state studies)
Includes bibliographical references and index.
Contents: Six flags of Texas -- Mexican Texas -- Republic of Texas --
The 28th state -- Progress in Texas.
 ISBN 1-4034-0687-1 -- ISBN 1-4034-2696-1
 1. Texas--History--Juvenile literature. [1. Texas--History.] I. Title. II. Series.
  F386.3.W35 2003
  976.4--dc21
 062011   2003009545
 0006204RP

Acknowledgments
The author and publishers are grateful to the following for permission to reproduce copyright material:

Cover photograph reproduced with permission of ©The Granger Collection, New York

pp. 28, 32, 33, 41 Corbis; **p. 4** Joseph Sohm/ChromoSohm Inc./Corbis; **pp. 5, 8, 11, 18, 21, 22, 36, 38** The Granger Collection, New York; **pp. 6, 10, 14, 15. 24, 39** Bettmann/Corbis; **pp. 9, 30** North Wind Picture Archive; **pp. 13, 17. 23,** Bob Daemmrich Photography, Inc.; **p. 19** State Preservation Board, Austin, Texas/The Surrender of Santa Anna/Photographer Unknown, pre 1991/CHA 1989.046/pre conservation; **p. 25** Lee Snider/Corbis; **p. 26** Tom Till/drr.net; **p. 29** Underwood & Underwood/Corbis; **p. 31** Brown Brothers; **p. 40** Reuters NewMedia, Inc./Corbis; **p. 43** Michael Stravato/AP Photo

Every effort has been made to contact copyright holders of any material reproduced in this book. Any omissions will be rectified in subsequent printings if notice is given to the publisher.

Disclaimer
All the Internet addresses (URLs) given in this book were valid at the time of going to press. However, due to the dynamic nature of the Internet, some addresses may have changed, or sites may have changed or ceased to exist since publication. While the author and publisher regret any inconvenience this may cause readers, no responsibility for any such changes can be accepted by either the author or the publisher.

Contents

Early Texas: Prehistory to 1800 4

Mexican Texas and
the Texas Revolution: 1800–1835 10

The Republic of Texas: 1836–1845 20

The 28th State: 1846–1875. 25

Progress in Texas: 1865–1900 33

The 20th Century and Beyond: 1900– 40

Map of Texas 44

Timeline 45

Glossary *46*

Find Out More *47*

Index *48*

Some words are shown in bold, **like this**. You can find out what they mean by looking in the glossary.

Early Texas: Prehistory to 1800

The human history of Texas stretches back over 11,000 years. The Paleo-Indians were the first to inhabit this vast land. In the 1500s, their Native American descendants met the Spaniards, who were looking for gold. The French, who were trying to expand their empire, also came to Texas. This is just the beginning of the history of Texas.

Early Native Americans: 9200 BCE–1500 CE

The first inhabitants of Texas were the Paleo-Indians. When they lived in Texas, the climate was much cooler than it is today. The Paleo-Indians survived by hunting mammoths, mastodons, and bison. By 6000 BCE, the Archaic Indians were living in Texas. The climate had become hotter and drier by that time. The Archaic Indians lived in rock shelters. They ate seeds, beans, and small animals such as rabbits and fish. The Archaics left behind examples of pictographs, or rock art.

These pictographs were made by Archaic Indians about 5,000 years ago near present-day Del Rio, Texas.

By 700 CE, several Native American groups were living in northeast Texas. These people, called the Caddo, were peaceful farmers who also hunted for bear and deer. The Caddo tattooed themselves, and often wore a **unique** type of black leather clothing. It was the Caddo that the Spanish encountered when they arrived in Texas in 1528.

The Spanish Conquistadors: 1528–1600

Spain was the first European nation to place a claim on Texas. Spain had several reasons for being interested in this part of the world. Spanish rulers sent **conquistadors** to look for precious gold. The conquistadors were permitted to keep four-fifths of what they found. The remaining one-fifth had to be sent to the Spanish ruler. Priests also came to convert Native Americans to **Christianity**. During the Spanish occupation, many Spaniards lost their lives without finding wealth. Many more Native Americans died from European diseases or from the cruel treatment they received from the Spaniards, who forced them to work.

This image shows Cabeza de Vaca on the shores of the Gulf of Mexico in 1528.

The first person to write about Texas in detail was Álvar Nûñez Cabeza de Vaca. He and 250 companions survived an **expedition** to the New World led by the Spaniard Pánfilo de Narváez. Their rafts were thrown onto the Texas coast by a storm in 1528. After eight years among Native American groups in Texas and Mexico, four survivors reached Mexico City.

Three hundred Spaniards and hundreds of Native Americans, along with horses, sheep, pigs, and cattle, accompanied Coronado on his search for the Seven Cities of Gold.

In Mexico the survivors told the authorities about the landforms, Native Americans, and resources they had seen. Although they did not tell stories about finding cities of gold, rumors about such places spread throughout Mexico City. Because of these rumors, Francisco de Coronado, a conquistador, led 1,000 soldiers on a mission in search of what legends called Cíbola, the Seven Cities of Gold.

Coronado marched north from Mexico City. He then headed east across the Texas Panhandle (see map on page 44), where he explored Palo Duro Canyon. He continued his search for the Seven Cities all the way into Kansas. When he did not find them, he returned to Mexico in 1542.

The Fate of the Four Survivors

Álvar Núñez Cabeza de Vaca returned to Spain and wrote about his adventures. Alonso del Castillo Maldonado and Andrés Dorantes de Carranza stayed in Mexico City and became wealthy landowners. Estevanico, a native of Morocco and Dorantes's slave, was sent north to find a path for the Spanish explorer Francisco de Coronado, who was looking for gold. Estevanico reached a **Zuñi pueblo** in southwest New Mexico believed to be the first of the Seven Cities of Gold. When Coronado reached the pueblo, he found that Estevanico had been killed outside the pueblo's walls. Estevanico is thought to have been the first African in Texas.

The First Missionaries: 1682

In 1682 **missionaries** from Spain established the first permanent European settlements in Texas near present-day El Paso. They wanted to force the local Native Americans to convert to Christianity. The missionaries hoped that by creating these **missions**, Spain's claim to the New World would be stronger. Between 1682 and 1793, 26 Spanish missions were built and run in different areas of Texas.

Missions in Spanish Texas: 1682–1800

Most Spanish missions were found along the Rio Grande and in South and East Texas.

The French: 1682–1685

In 1682 French explorer René-Robert Cavelier, Sieur de La Salle, landed on the southeast coast of Texas. He had traveled down the Mississippi River from Illinois. La Salle claimed the land for France and named the territory La Louisiane in honor of French king Louis XIV.

In 1685 La Salle returned to the area with a group of 200 French colonists. They built Fort St. Louis on Garcitas Creek (see map on page 7). After arriving, La Salle explored more of the area. But the French colonists met with many difficulties. Most of them died from disease, malnutrition, or encounters with the Karankawa Indians who lived along the coast. In 1687 La Salle was murdered by his own frustrated and desperate men.

This 1698 engraving shows La Salle's ship, the *Belle*. In real life, the masts of the ship were much shorter.

The *Belle*

In 1995 **archaeologists** found the remains of the Belle, La Salle's ship. They **restored** many of the ship's **artifacts**. At Garcitas Creek they found eight French cannons. In 2000 they found the bones of two people. These are probably the bones of French settlers that the Spaniards buried after finding them at the site of the original French fort, Fort St. Louis.

More Spanish Missions: 1716–1755

The French settlement in Texas was unsuccessful, but it alarmed Spain. In 1716 Spain started to build missions in East Texas to make its claim secure. Mission San Antonio de Valero, now known as the Alamo, was built two years later as a midway point to these missions. Some East Texas missions were removed to San Antonio about 15 years later. Four missions along the San Antonio River—San José, Concepción, San Juan Capistrano, and Espada—are now a part of the National Park System.

Another mission called Espíritu Santo was founded in 1722 near the site of La Salle's settlement on Matagorda Bay. In 1749 it was moved to La Bahia or Goliad on the lower San Antonio River. It is now a state park.

The Alamo

Mission San Antonio de Valero, established in 1718, is known today as the Alamo. *Alamo* is the Spanish word for "cottonwood tree." Cottonwoods may have grown nearby, or the name may refer to soldiers from Álamo de Parras, Coahuila, Mexico, who occupied the mission in 1803.

Mexican Texas and the Texas Revolution: 1800–1835

The **missions** the Spanish built to discourage French settlement could not save them from the biggest threat to their rule: Mexican independence. If the Mexican colonists were to declare their independence—as American colonists did during the American Revolution (1775–1783)—Spain would no longer have a claim to Texas.

Mexican Independence

Mexicans first declared their liberty from Spain on September 16, 1810. But it wasn't until 1821 that Mexico actually gained its independence. Texas, now a part of Mexico, was joined with Coahuila as the state of Coahuila y Tejas.

Agustín de Iturbide fought for Mexican independence from Spain. He became the first emperor of Mexico, but was later exiled.

The Empresario System

In January 1821, an American named Moses Austin came to San Antonio from Missouri to ask Mexico's permission to bring American settlers into Texas. Moses Austin died six months later, and his son, Stephen Fuller Austin, finalized a settlement contract with the new Mexican government. **Anglo-Americans** quickly started colonizing Texas.

Stephen Fuller Austin was born in Virginia and studied law in Louisiana before moving to Texas in 1821.

Mexico developed the *empresario* system to attract settlers to Texas to form a barrier against raids from Native Americans. This system gave a land grant, or large piece of land, to *empresarios* who paid a small fee for the **title** to the land. The *empresario* brought in settlers and had full responsibility for their welfare and behavior. The *empresario* received no pay for the job, but was given about 22,000 acres (8,900 hectares) of land for every 100 colonists who came. A settler family received a league of land, which was 4,428 acres (1,792 hectares), to graze cattle and a labor of land, which was 177 acres (72 hectares), to cultivate land. Single men received 1,107 acres (448 hectares). Twenty-eight *empresario* grants were issued, but not all fulfilled their contracts in the six-year time limit. Several colonies had severe problems.

By 1836, 35,000 people were living in Texas. Stephen Fuller Austin was the most successful *empresario*. He issued 1,540 land titles from his headquarters in San Felipe de Austin. He explored the land and carefully recorded land ownership. Austin learned Spanish so that he could translate the law for his settlers. He also went to Mexico to meet with authorities to make sure his colonies received good treatment.

All the *empresarios* were American except for one married couple from Mexico. Doña Patricia de la Garza De León and her husband Martín De León, both **Tejanos**, founded the town Victoria in 1824. Doña De León invested $10,000 to help start the colony. The De Leóns were the first large cattle ranchers in Texas, and their **brand** was the first registered in the state. When Martín De León died in 1833, he left behind $500,000, making Doña De León the wealthiest person in Texas. During the Texas Revolution, members of the De León family fought with Texas and donated supplies to use against the Mexican government. After the revolution, however, Texans turned against the Tejanos. Doña De León lost all her property.

Native Americans in Texas

At the same time as Anglo-American settlers were moving into Texas, peaceful Cherokee, Shawnee, and Delaware Indians moved into the area north of Nacogdoches. The Alabama and Coushatta Indians moved into southeast Texas. They were forced into Texas by Anglo settlers who had pushed them off their land in the east.

Conflicts with Mexico: 1830–1835

As more Anglo-American settlers came to Texas, the Mexican government grew more alarmed at their behavior. Slavery was forbidden in Mexico, but Texas planters brought in great numbers of slaves. The planters not only thought it was their right to have slaves, but they felt that their way of farming relied upon it. Slavery became the major source of problems between the Anglos and the Mexican government. Settlers also ignored other Mexican laws that they did not like. Mexico suspected that the United States wanted to **annex** Texas, and so the Mexican congress passed the Decree of April 6, 1830. The decree said that no more Americans could enter Texas. A new tax on goods coming from the United States made trade impossible. These new laws upset the settlers.

Texans met in San Felipe in 1833 and prepared a **constitution** that separated Texas from Coahuila. When Stephen Fuller Austin took the Texas Constitution to Mexico to be approved by the Mexican congress, he was arrested and held for two years. Austin returned to Texas in 1835 and called **delegates** together at Washington-on-the-Brazos. His years in Mexico had caused him to give up hope for a peaceful existence with Mexico.

The Texas Revolution: 1835–1836

In October 1835, the first shot of the Texas Revolution was fired in Gonzales, the westernmost town of Anglo-American settlement (see map on page 16). A small force of Mexican soldiers from San Antonio came to retrieve a cannon that the Mexican government had given to the colonists. After a brief **skirmish**, the Mexican soldiers retreated. Following the battle, angry Texans who had gathered to defend the cannon marched to San Antonio. They were joined by volunteers from around the United States.

"Come and Take It" Flag

When Mexican soldiers arrived in Gonzales to take the town cannon, Texans challenged them to "come and take it." After a brief skirmish, the Mexican soldiers left without the cannon. Sara Seely DeWitt, who had started DeWitt's colony with her *empresario* husband Green DeWitt, made the "Come and Take It" flag with her daughter Naomi. To make the flag, they cut up Naomi's wedding dress. The flag was white with a black cannon on it. It became a battle flag of the Texas Revolution.

The Texans attacked San Antonio. They forced Mexican Commander Martín Perfecto de Cos—brother-in-law of Antonio López de Santa Anna, president of Mexico—to leave the city with his soldiers. Cos promised never to return, and the Texans celebrated. They did not count on Santa Anna's anger.

Sam Houston, the commander of the Texas army, sent James Bowie with a small force to San Antonio in January 1836. If the city could not be defended, Bowie had been told to go back to Gonzales. Bowie stayed, and William Travis arrived with soldiers on February 3. Five days later, David Crockett rode into San Antonio with a dozen fighters from Tennessee. Travis and Bowie shared command of the 184 men gathered there.

The townspeople of San Antonio did not believe that the Mexican army would attack during winter, so news of the approaching Mexican forces sent them scrambling into the Alamo. Santa Anna had marched his army through a rare winter storm in northern Mexico. Cos and his army were with them. Santa Anna arrived in San Antonio on February 23 with about 2,000 soldiers. He hoisted a blood-red flag to show that there would be no surrender. The Texans answered him with a cannon shot.

The army of Santa Anna (above) was larger than that of the Texans, but many of his troops were poorly equipped or were prisoners of war who were being forced to fight.

The battle for the Alamo was very important because it blocked one of two major roads leading from Mexico into Texas. If the Alamo fell, Mexican troops could more easily advance into Texas.

The following day, Bowie, who was very ill, turned his command over to Travis. That night, messengers slipped out of the Alamo under cover of darkness with a desperate appeal for help from Travis. The only volunteers who came were 32 men from Gonzales. They entered the Alamo before dawn on March 1. They and the other volunteers stood at their places. But Mexican forces, which had increased to over 3,000 and would eventually reach up to 6,000, kept firing cannons at the Alamo. Those inside had no way of knowing that delegates meeting at Washington-on-the-Brazos had already signed the Texas Declaration of Independence.

A Gift to a Little Girl

William Travis knew he was not likely to survive the **siege** of the Alamo. Almaron Dickinson, one of the Alamo defenders, had brought his wife and two-year-old daughter Angelina inside the compound. Travis gave his **cat's-eye** ring to Angelina. The ring is now on display in the Alamo.

Before dawn on March 6, wave after wave of Mexican soldiers climbed over their own dead to scale the north wall of the Alamo. By daybreak, all the defenders were dead. Santa Anna interviewed the survivors—all women, children, or slaves—and sent them away. Susanna Dickinson was told to go to Gonzales and describe the fate that awaited other Texans who rebelled.

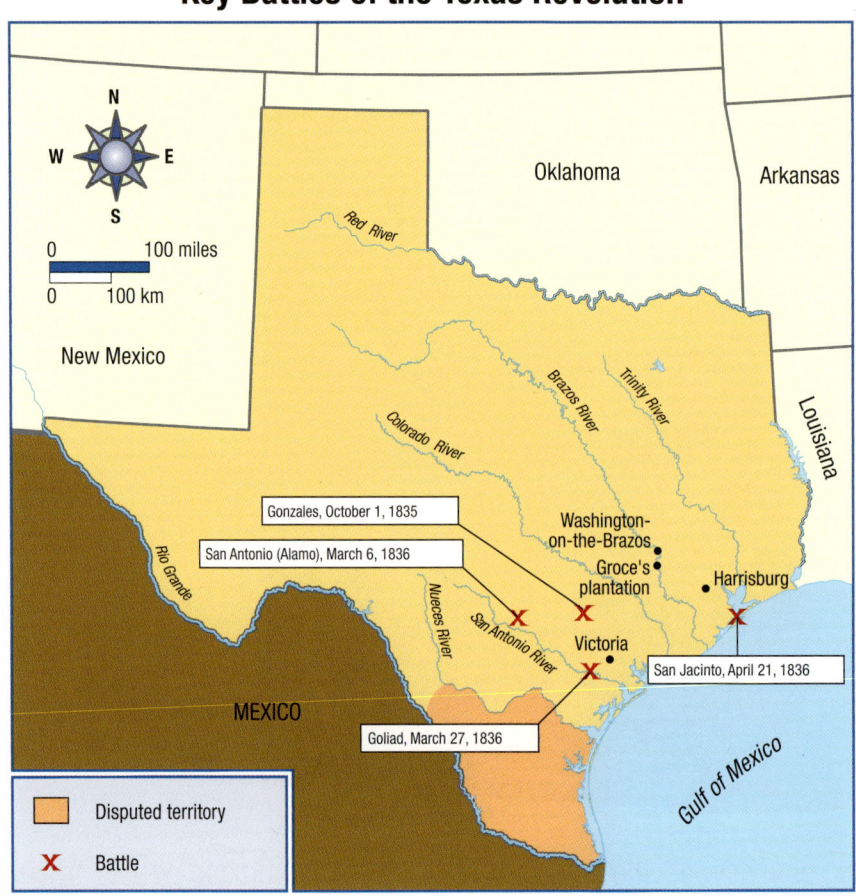

Key Battles of the Texas Revolution

The Texas Declaration of Independence

While the Alamo was under siege, **delegates** to the Convention of 1836 met in Washington-on-the-Brazos to write the Texas Declaration of Independence. On March 2, delegates signed the Declaration. The Declaration stated the reasons why Texas should no longer be governed by Mexico. It listed many **grievances** Texans had suffered. Then it declared that Texas was independent from Mexico.

Alamo Burial

The body of Gregorio Esparza, a **Tejano** who fought for Texan independence, was claimed by his brother and buried. Esparza was the only defender of the Alamo to be buried. After Santa Anna had viewed the bodies of Travis, Bowie, and Crockett, he ordered all the others to be burned.

Delegates then began work on a **constitution**. During this time, Sam Houston, commander in chief of the Texas army, left for Gonzales. He was organizing the army there when Susanna Dickinson arrived with news of the defeat at the Alamo. Houston burned Gonzales so that the Mexican army could not use its supplies. He began a retreat and sent word for the 400 men at Goliad to join him in Victoria. James Walker Fannin Jr., commander at Goliad, hesitated. Nearly all of his troops were captured and **executed** by the Mexican army.

Houston retreated again. At the Colorado River his army increased to 1,300. All around them, panicked settlers were fleeing to the United States. The **interim** Texas officials, including President David Burnet and Vice President Lorenzo de Zavala, had moved east to Harrisburg.

By March 27, Houston had pulled back to the Brazos and was camped across the river from Jared Groce's **plantation**. Groce supplied food, medicine, and arms. For two weeks, the Texans trained to be soldiers. Constant rain made life miserable. Many were ill, and others left in disgust over Houston's retreats. They wanted to fight. The only bright spot was that two cannons, called the Twin Sisters, had been sent by citizens of Cincinnati, Ohio.

The original Twin Sisters arrived in Galveston in 1836. No one knows if they still exist today, but **replicas** can be seen at the Texas Military Forces Museum in Austin.

Gail Borden was named the official printer of the new republic. He printed the Texas Declaration of Independence.

When the Texans crossed the flooded Brazos, still headed east, they reached a fork in the road northwest of Harrisburg. The east road led to safety in Louisiana. The south road led to Harrisburg and the enemy. A shout went up as the men took the road to Harrisburg.

Santa Anna ignored the force from Groce's **plantation** and went after the Texas officials in Harrisburg. When he arrived on April 17, the town was deserted except for three newspaper printers. They were putting out an edition of the *Telegraph and Texas Register*, Gail Borden's newspaper. Santa Anna ordered that the press be dumped into Buffalo Bayou. It was later pulled out and was used to start the newspaper that became the *Houston Post*, which was published until 1995.

The printers told Santa Anna that Texas officials had just left. About 700 Mexican troops chased them to Galveston Bay. Santa Anna, satisfied that he had cut off the Texas army from its government, returned to the San Jacinto River. Houston learned of Santa Anna's small force. On the morning of April 20, 1836, the Texans hid and waited for the Mexicans. A short **skirmish** took place.

The next morning, General Cos arrived with 500 more Mexican soldiers. The Mexican soldiers went about camp duties, because they assumed there would be no fighting that day. Santa Anna rested under a tree.

Tejanos at San Jacinto

When Sam Houston suggested that the 20 **Tejanos** led by Juan Seguín guard the army's baggage during the Battle of San Jacinto, Seguín reacted angrily. He and his men wanted to fight. Five of the seven Tejanos who had died defending the Alamo were from his company. The Tejanos had as much to lose as the Texans if Santa Anna's forces were not defeated. During the battle, the Tejanos wore cardboard in their hats so that their comrades would not think they were a part of the Mexican army and shoot them by mistake.

Juan Seguín became the only Tejano to be elected to the senate of the Republic. Unfortunately, he was later pressured to leave Texas by **Anglos** who falsely accused him of **conspiring** with the Mexican government to return control of Texas to Mexico.

The Battle of San Jacinto: April 21, 1836

At mid-afternoon, the Texans approached behind a slight rise in the land and formed a line. At 4:30 p.m., Houston, mounted on a white stallion named Saracen, signaled with his sword to fire. The Twin Sisters boomed and **cavalry**, under the command of Mirabeau B. Lamar, charged. The Texans fired. Without stopping to reload, they charged ahead swinging rifles and Bowie knives. Cries of "Remember the Alamo! Remember Goliad!" filled the air. The Mexican line fell back in confusion. Those who retreated into the nearby lagoon were drowned or shot. The battle lasted only eighteen minutes. It was the last battle of the Texas Revolution, and Texas was free.

Santa Anna was not found until the day after the battle. He was wearing a common soldier's outfit, but underneath it he wore a silk shirt with **diamond studs**. His captors realized who he was when Mexican prisoners called out "*el presidente*"—the president—as he passed. Santa Anna asked to be taken to Houston, who lay under a tree with a bullet-shattered ankle. Cries went up to hang the Mexican general. Instead, Houston bargained with Santa Anna—his life in exchange for a letter ordering the Mexicans to retreat. The new Republic of Texas was born.

Sam Houston traveled to New Orleans after the Battle of San Jacinto to receive medical treatment for his ankle.

The Republic of Texas: 1836–1845

Following the Battle of San Jacinto, Santa Anna was taken to meet with Texas officials. Three weeks after the battle, he signed two treaties. In the Treaty of Velasco, Santa Anna promised never again to take up arms against Texas. All fighting would stop, prisoners would be exchanged, and Mexican troops would withdraw beyond the Rio Grande. The second treaty was to be kept a secret until its terms were met. In that treaty, Santa Anna pledged to support Texas independence, create a trade agreement, and recognize the Rio Grande as the Texas-Mexico border.

But against the orders of the new Texas government, the Texas army did not release Santa Anna. The Mexican government did not wish to recognize Texas independence or the boundary lines named in the Treaty of Velasco. Therefore, Mexico rejected the treaties.

Despite Mexican rejection of Texas independence, Texas did become a republic. As a republic, Texas had a president to head the government. David Burnet served as **interim** president until the first election was held. Presidents served for three years, but could not serve two terms in a row. Three men held office from 1836 to 1846: Sam Houston, who was elected twice, Mirabeau Lamar, and Anson Jones. These men helped the new republic through its problems and celebrated its successes.

Interim Texas Officials

David Burnet, born in New Jersey, was originally an *empresario* near Nacogdoches. On March 10, 1836, he was elected interim president of the new Texas republic.

Manuel Lorenzo Justiniano de Zavala y Sáenz was originally from southern Mexico. He, too, had been an *empresario*. Zavala was a representative at the Convention of 1836, where his fellow **delegates** elected him interim vice president of the new republic.

Stephen Austin and the New Republic

During the first months of the republic, Stephen Austin worked as **Secretary of State**. He tried to persuade other countries to recognize Texas as an independent nation. Austin spoke his last words just before he died of **pneumonia** on December 27, 1836. **Delirious**, he said, "Texas recognized … Did you see it in the paper?" He believed that the United States had recognized Texas as an independent nation. In reality, that did not happen until 1837.

Sam Houston: 1836–1838

Sam Houston, the hero of the Battle of San Jacinto, became the first president of the Republic of Texas on October 22, 1836. His time in office was very difficult. The new republic faced huge debts. Native Americans, believing that whites were invading their territory, at times attacked frontier settlements. And Texas was under the constant threat of invasion by Mexico, which still did not recognize Texas independence.

During Houston's first term as president, he tried hard to avoid problems between settlers and Native Americans. He also tried, unsuccessfully, to have Texas **annexed** to the United States. In 1836 the town of Houston was founded and became the capital of Texas. Houston left office because he could not be elected again at that time.

The colors on the flag of the Republic of Texas have meaning. Red stands for bravery, white for purity, and blue for loyalty.

Mirabeau B. Lamar: 1838–1841

Mirabeau B. Lamar, who had been vice president under Houston, was elected the second president of the Republic of Texas in 1838. He is often called the Father of Texas Education because he set aside land for public schools and a university. In 1839 he moved the capital from Houston to Austin.

Whereas Houston had a policy of friendship and cooperation with the Native Americans, Lamar wanted to drive them from Texas. He ordered all Native Americans to leave Texas. Most were never paid for their land or crops. Lamar also opposed the annexation of Texas by the United States, and wanted to extend the republic's borders. By the end of Lamar's presidency, the republic had almost no money left.

Mirabeau Lamar was born in Georgia. He moved to Texas in 1835.

Timeline of Republic of Texas Presidents

March 1836–October 1836	David Burnet (interim president)
October 1836–December 1838	Sam Houston
December 1838–December 1841	Mirabeau Lamar
December 1841–December 1844	Sam Houston
December 1844–February 1846	Anson Jones

Sam Houston's Second Term: 1841–1844

Houston easily won reelection in 1841. He put the Republic of Texas on a strict **budget**. He again worked for peace between settlers and Native Americans and made treaties with the Native American groups still living in Texas. During Houston's term, Mexico invaded Texas, but he was able to avoid another war.

When Mexico invaded in 1842, Houston ordered that the archives, or government papers, be removed from Austin, a place he believed was too open to attack. However, an Austin boardinghouse owner named Angelina Eberly noticed the archives being taken. She fired a cannon to alert the town's citizens. The people of Austin did not want the archives removed because they wanted Austin to remain the capital. They prevented the archives from leaving their city. The State Archives Building today is across the street from the capitol in Austin.

The Lorenzo de Zavala State Archives Building in Austin is named for the first vice president of the Republic of Texas.

Anson Jones: 1844–1846

Anson Jones, known as the **Architect** of **Annexation**, became president in 1844. During his presidency, Jones was able to persuade the Mexican government to recognize Texas independence. Once that happened, Jones offered Texans two options. They could enjoy a peaceful relationship with Mexico and remain an independent republic. Or, they could accept an offer of annexation from the United States. Texans chose annexation.

The annexation agreement pledged the United States to defend the Rio Grande as the boundary with Mexico. Texas turned over the defense of its forts to the United States, but kept its public lands as well as its debt. It also was given the right to divide into five states.

Texans approved a state **constitution**, and on December 29, 1845, President James K. Polk signed the act that made Texas the 28th state. On February 19, 1846, Anson Jones declared, "The final act in this great drama is now performed: the Republic of Texas is no more." Veterans of San Jacinto shed tears as the Lone Star Flag of Texas was lowered and replaced by the flag of the United States.

President Jones took down the flag of the Republic of Texas during a ceremony on February 19, 1846. The flag of the United States was raised in its place.

The 28th State: 1846–1875

Thousands of immigrants moved to Texas after it joined the United States. This home was built by German settlers near Castroville in 1850.

As promised when Texas was annexed, U.S. President James Polk sent troops to defend the Rio Grande and enforce it as the boundary with Mexico. But Mexico claimed that the Nueces River, not the Rio Grande, was the Texas–Mexico boundary. The Mexican government considered the presence of U.S. troops near the Rio Grande to be an act of aggression, and it declared war. The first two battles of the Mexican War (1846–1848) took place near Brownsville. United States General Winfield Scott then captured Mexico City. The Treaty of Guadalupe Hidalgo, signed on February 2, 1848, ended the war.

As a result of the treaty, Mexico lost all of the land that is now California, Nevada, and Utah. It also lost almost all of Arizona and New Mexico, as well as parts of Colorado and Wyoming. Texas had long claimed land reaching to the upper Rio Grande. This included half of New Mexico and parts of Colorado, Wyoming, Kansas, and Oklahoma. The Compromise of 1850 shrank Texas to its present-day borders. In return, the United States government paid Texas $10 million to cover its debts. But even with less land, there was still room for large numbers of arriving Swedish, Czech, German, and Polish **immigrants** to find a home in Texas.

Fort Davis was built in 1854 to protect settlers and travelers. The site has been restored, and today visitors can experience what it might have been like to live at the fort during the 1850s.

Texas Forts

The United States government established forts to defend Texas frontier settlements against Native Americans. The Native Americans were alarmed at the increasing number of whites moving onto their land. The line of forts stretched from the Red River in the north of Texas to the Rio Grande in the south. But the forts soon became useless, as the settlers they were supposed to protect moved beyond them. Some forts are crumbled ruins today. Others, such as Fort Worth and Fort Stockton, grew into cities. Some, like Fort Davis and Fort Concho in San Angelo, have been **restored**. Some are still active. After 1946, Fort Bliss in El Paso became the United States Army's air defense headquarters.

Fort Mason

During the mid–1800s, Texas was a training ground for the United States military. Twenty Civil War generals came from Fort Mason (1848–1869). Twelve of them became Confederate officers, and eight of them fought for the Union. Robert E. Lee was at the fort when he was called to Washington, D.C., and offered command of the Union forces. Instead, he decided to lead the Confederate army.

Confederate Texas and the Civil War: 1860–1865

By 1860, the United States was quickly approaching a **crisis**. The North and the South were bitterly divided on the issue of slavery. Many people in the North felt that slavery should be outlawed. The Southern economy, however, depended heavily on slave labor. The industrial North wanted more money to develop its roads and businesses. But the South wanted the government to spend more money developing its agricultural **exports**. Southern states started to talk about **seceding** from the United States in order to start their own country.

In 1860 one-third of the 600,000 people living in Texas were slaves. Owners of the cotton **plantations** that were concentrated in the eastern part of the state strongly supported a move to secede from the United States. Texans on smaller farms in North Texas did not depend on slaves and did not favor secession.

Sam Houston, who was elected governor after serving 13 years as a Texas senator, tried to keep Texas in the **Union**. But in March 1861, the majority of Texans voted to join the **Confederate** States of America. State officials were required to take an oath of loyalty to the new government. Houston refused to take the oath. Edward Clark stepped into the governor's office, and the Confederate flag flew over the state capitol.

Texas contributed food, money, and soldiers to the Confederacy. Texans fought in major Civil War battles in Virginia, Tennessee, and Mississippi, as well as on the Texas borders. At one point, Galveston and Brownsville were actually lost to Union forces, but Texas forces soon recovered their cities.

On January 1, 1863, Confederate forces surprised the Union army, which controlled Galveston Harbor. Union ships were forced to leave, and the Confederates controlled the port for the rest of the war.

During the Civil War, Sam Houston retired to Huntsville. Native Americans appealed to him when their sons were drafted into the Confederate army, and he was able to stop the practice. Houston was a strong believer in the United States **Constitution**. When he learned of President Abraham Lincoln's **Emancipation Proclamation** in 1863, he set his slaves free while most slave owners ignored the proclamation.

News of the Confederate surrender in April 1865 did not reach Texas right away. On May 13, 1865, the last battle of the Civil War took place at Palmito Ranch near Brownsville. John "Rip" Ford's forces defeated Union troops. The United States flag again flew over Texas.

Juneteenth

Union Major General Gordon Granger arrived in Galveston on June 19, 1865. When he read the Emancipation Proclamation that freed the slaves, huge celebrations broke out. Juneteenth became a holiday of parades, speeches, and family gatherings. It is still celebrated in Texas today.

But not all African Americans in Texas received information about the end of the war. Many whites kept the news about emancipation from African Americans on purpose, and some Texas African Americans were held in slavery even after Juneteenth.

The Start of Reconstruction: 1865

Reconstruction began with the end of the Civil War. During this time, soldiers were sent into Texas to ensure the rights of freed slaves. Few people had money, and it was a difficult time for almost all Texans.

Although now free, African Americans had a particularly hard time. While slaves, few African Americans had been permitted to learn skills that would provide them with good wages, so it was hard for them to make a living. The United States government set up the Freedmen's Bureau to help them get fair wages. The bureau also provided schools for former slaves who had been denied the right to an education.

Buffalo Soldiers

After the Civil War (1861–1865), African-American soldiers—including the Ninth and Tenth **Cavalry**—served at frontier Texas forts. Plains Indians called them "Buffalo Soldiers," possibly because of the strength and courage they showed in battle.

After Slavery

Even though new laws gave former slaves rights on paper, African Americans had trouble exercising these rights in real life.

Whites often used violence to keep African Americans from leaving their sharecropping jobs and from voting. Between 1865 and 1868, more than 350 of 1,500 acts of violence were murders of African-American men. African Americans continued to struggle for their rights for the next 100 years.

Freed slaves owned no land. In order to make a living, many returned to their previous masters as paid laborers. Many freedmen and poor white farmers worked as sharecroppers. White farm owners supplied land, seed, and tools for the sharecroppers. The sharecroppers then worked to raise a crop. When the crop was harvested, the owner took half of it. Under this system, sharecroppers barely earned a living.

Six African Americans were elected to a statewide convention whose job was to write a new Texas constitution. When the constitution was finished in 1869, Texas was readmitted to the Union. Many Texans disliked the power that Texas governors had been given, so another constitution was written in 1876. It limited the power of the governor. This constitution, changed many times, is still in use today.

Most sharecroppers in post–Civil War Texas were African American. These sharecroppers picked cotton to earn their living.

Renewed Native American Conflicts: 1870s

By the mid-1800s, only a few groups of Native Americans still lived in Texas, including the Tonkawa, the Apache, the Kiowa, the Kiowa Apache, and the Comanche. It is estimated that between 1528 and 1890, diseases killed more than 90 percent of all Native Americans in Texas. Most of the others were forced to leave their homes by settlers hungry for more land.

General William T. Sherman, commanding general of the United States army, made an inspection of Texas forts in 1871. He was convinced there were no longer hostile Native American groups. But then, the lone survivor of an attack on a wagon train stumbled into a frontier fort with news of an ambush by 100 Kiowa, Comanche, and other Native Americans. General Sherman arrested Kiowa Chiefs Satank, Satanta, and Big Tree. They were tried in Jacksboro and found guilty of the attack.

William T. Sherman was a major general in the Union army during the Civil War.

This photo shows Apache Indians on the Southern Pacific Railroad near the Nueces River. They are being taken to reservations.

In order to force other Native Americans onto **reservations**, General Sherman set out to destroy Texas's bison. The Native Americans depended on bison in order to live. They were furious at Sherman and the settlers, and fought back. Sherman then ordered 2,000 soldiers and scouts from New Mexico, Kansas, Oklahoma, and Texas to meet in the upper Red River area to **subdue** the Native Americans. Colonel Ranald Mackenzie, called Bad Hand by the Native Americans because he had lost two fingers, led one band of troops from Fort Concho. His troops caught up with the Comanche and Kiowa in Palo Duro Canyon and slaughtered all 1,000 of their horses. This forced Chief Quanah Parker and his warriors to surrender in June 1875, bringing an end to the **Red River Wars**.

Progress in Texas: 1865–1900

In the late 1800s, with the **plantation culture** in decline, Texans looked for new ways to develop their land and earn a living. Railroads led to the development of new settlements and made it possible for Texans to ship their goods to other states. The cattle business grew quickly. And the discovery of oil changed the history of Texas—and the world—forever.

Railroads and Economic Growth

Railroads played an important part in getting Texas products to market. They also led settlers to new areas. Before the arrival of railroads, the great majority of Texans lived in East Texas or along the Gulf Coast. Railroads also influenced the growth of cities and towns by selling lots. Towns sprang up along the routes. Ten years after the railroad reached El Paso, the city's population grew from 700 to 10,000.

Railroad depots became busy places where goods were shipped all over the country. Below, cotton is being shipped from the Texas Central Railway Yards in Houston.

Jefferson, Texas

Jefferson was a thriving northeast Texas port. Railroad **magnate** Jay Gould warned the town that it would not be able to survive if it did not accept his railroad. Citizens of Jefferson refused his offer. The railroad passed Jefferson by, and no new development came to the area. Today, Jefferson's Victorian houses and buildings are a tourist attraction.

The first railroad in Texas was the Buffalo Bayou, Brazos and Colorado Railway. It ran from Houston to Stafford. Those 20 miles (32 kilometers) of track were the second railroad line west of the Mississippi River, and they are still in use by the Southern Pacific Railroad. To encourage the railroad companies to build more track, the state gave them public land. By 1882, railroad companies had received 30 million acres (12,140,570 hectares).

The Heyday of the Cattle Trails: 1866–1890

Cattle were first brought to Texas by the Spaniards during the **mission** days. They thrived on the plentiful grass. After **Anglo** settlers arrived, Spanish cattle mixed with Anglo cattle, and the longhorn was born. Longhorn cattle reached huge numbers during the Civil War. In 1866 more than 200,000 longhorns were driven to the nearest railroads in St. Joseph, Missouri. But settlers grew angry because the longhorns trampled their crops. The longhorns were banned when it was discovered that they transported ticks that carried Texas Fever, a disease to which they were **immune** but that killed the settlers' cattle.

Cattle Trails and Texas Forts

To avoid driving cattle through settled areas, railroad companies extended their tracks to Abilene, Kansas, and built holding pens for the longhorns. The cattle then made the long trip to the railroad over trails with plentiful grass and without upsetting settlers. The most famous trail was **blazed** by Jesse Chisholm. The Chisholm Trail ran from south Texas, across **Indian Territory**, to Abilene, Kansas. It had many branches, reaching all the way down to the Rio Grande, but it was all known simply as the Chisholm Trail. Five million head of cattle were herded to the trains along the Chisholm Trail.

This engraving shows cowboys herding Texas longhorns onto a boxcar at Abilene, Texas, in 1871.

As settlers pushed westward, the trails moved farther west to avoid them. The Western Trail ran from Fort Griffin to Ellsworth, or Dodge City, Kansas. Charles Goodnight and his partner, Oliver Loving, opened another trail that took cattle to ranches in New Mexico and Colorado. The Goodnight-Loving Trail swung west to the Horsehead Crossing on the Pecos River, north of Fort Stockton, and followed the river into New Mexico.

Old Blue

After a few days on the trail, cattle settled into a steady pace that carried them about 12 miles (19 kilometers) a day. On the trail, certain steers took the lead. A big steer with dark horns named Old Blue set the pace when a rancher named Charles Goodnight drove the first herd from his Palo Duro ranch to Dodge City. At the rail line, Old Blue stepped aside. The rest of the herd filled the cattle cars, but he trotted back down the trail with the cowboys. Goodnight was very fond of Old Blue, who led eight trail drives. The steer's horns were mounted on a plaque in Goodnight's ranch headquarters.

Women On the Trail

Women also worked in the cattle business. Some women inherited ranches when their husbands died. Some set up their own ranches. Elizabeth Ellen Johnson Williams put together her own herd before she married. She was a school teacher who kept records for cattlemen and recognized the profits to be made. She registered her own brand in 1871 and took her herd up the Chisholm Trail. In those days, marriage gave all of a wife's property to her husband. Before Lizzie and Hezekiah Williams married, he signed an agreement giving her control of her own finances and the ownership of her private property. When she died in 1924, she was worth nearly $250,000.

Longhorn cattle were ideal for trail drives. They had long legs, hard hooves, and were even able to gain weight along the way. A trail herd usually had 2,000 to 3,000 cattle handled by 10 or 11 cowboys. The trail driver received about one dollar per steer when the cattle reached the railroad. Cowboys, often in their teens, had a fixed wage. Others in the group—such as the cook or the wrangler, who kept the extra horses—might be older.

The job of a cowboy was difficult and dangerous. Days driving cattle on the trail were often boring. When storms caused **stampedes**, riders could be forced to stay in the saddle for three days, stopping only to eat. Trail herds became mixed during stampedes, and official counters kept **brand** books so that they could identify which cattle belonged in a herd. River crossings were especially difficult because of quicksand or swift currents that developed after rainstorms. Cowboys riding their best swimmer urged lead steers into the water, and others followed. If any turned back, riders and cattle could be drowned in the confusion.

This is an 1876 advertisement for Glidden's barbed wire. Its popularity with farmers led to the end of the cattle drives.

Trail drives lasted from 1866 to 1890, but the drives slowed during the 1880s because of **quarantines** against tick-carrying Texas cattle. The end came after barbed wire was patented in 1874 by Joseph R. Glidden. Glidden's invention was intended to keep cattle out of farmers' crops. In effect, barbed wire put an end to cattle drives.

Texas Oil

Oil wells rival cattle as a symbol of Texas. The state's first commercial well was drilled in 1894 in Corsicana, south of Dallas, by a company looking for water. That oil well was important because its commercial success led others to look for more oil fields. Today, Texas leads all other states in oil production.

Oil spews high into the air from the top of a Texas oil derrick.

The 20th Century and Beyond: 1900–

The new century had barely begun when the deadliest storm in the nation's history struck the city of Galveston (see map on page 44). An estimated 6,000 people died in a hurricane that raged from September 8 through September 9, 1900. As a result of the storm, a port was built farther inland. Buffalo Bayou was dredged, and the Port of Houston opened about 50 miles (81 kilometers) from the Gulf of Mexico. Today, the port handles the second largest amount of cargo in the nation.

A horse hauls away a cart of debris created by the hurricane of 1900.

The Importance of Oil

Texas businessman Patillo Higgins believed that Spindletop **salt dome** near Beaumont contained oil. He organized the Gladys City Company, whose purpose was to find oil in the dome. On January 10, 1901, oil came gushing out of the well with such force that drilling rods flew 100 feet (31 meters) into the air. An estimated 100,000 barrels of oil a day spewed unchecked for ten days. The success at Spindletop changed the focus of the Texas economy from agriculture to oil-related products.

The Permian Basin, stretching from West Texas to southeastern New Mexico, was developed during the 1920s. In the 1930s, the wells there were producing a huge amount of the world's total oil supply. In 1930 Marion "Dad" Joiner brought in a new well near Henderson, Texas. That well opened the huge East Texas oil field. In the rush to get oil, wells were drilled so close together that the legs of the **derricks** touched. The development of new oil wells created jobs. Many men who formerly had made their living as sharecroppers now found employment on drilling rigs.

First Female Governor

In 1914 a politician named James Ferguson was elected Texas governor. He was popular with farmers and helped put free textbooks in the public schools. After being charged with misuse of public money in 1917, he was **impeached** and removed from office. His wife, Miriam A. Wallace Ferguson, was elected governor in 1924. She was the first female governor of Texas. She fought the **Ku Klux Klan**, which controlled major Texas cities at the time, and pardoned many criminals. She was elected again in 1932, after several years out of office. She worked hard to help people during the Great Depression.

The Great Depression: 1929

During the **Great Depression**, many people were without jobs. Banks closed, and many Texans lost their life savings. The government tried to provide work for unemployed people. Participants in one project created post office murals, or large paintings. People working on another project gathered information about the state's **culture**. Yet another, the Civilian Conservation Corps (CCC), provided jobs for 50,000 Texans from 1933 to 1942. CCC workers improved farming conditions, worked in forestry, and built parks.

Men and women stand in line to receive food in San Antonio during the Great Depression.

Texas Centennial

In 1936 Texas celebrated its centennial, or 100th birthday. More than 6 million people attended an **exhibition** in Dallas. A 570-foot (174-meter) monument was built on the San Jacinto battleground east of Houston. Historic buildings and forts were **restored**. The United States Post Office issued a special three-cent stamp with images of Texas for the occasion.

World War II: 1939–1945

In December 1941, the United States entered World War II. World War II had been raging in Europe since 1939. But America's leaders had not wanted to get involved if they could avoid doing so.

During the war, Fort Worth and Dallas became major centers for aircraft manufacturing. Texans left farms and went to work in these city factories. For the first time in Texas history, thousands of women also left their homes and worked in factories. Texas coastal refineries produced fuel for planes, cars, and ships. The money Texans made in these new jobs helped the state recover from the Great Depression.

When the war started, thousands of soldiers trained at Texas military bases. The world's largest naval air training station was developed at Corpus Christi (see map on page 44). By the end of the war, 750,000 Texans, including 12,000 women, had served in the armed forces. During the war, 22,022 Texans were killed or died of wounds they received.

The Post-War Era

In the years following World War II, more businesses found a home in Texas. The state became a leader in the electronics, aerospace, and high-tech industries. In 1964 NASA (National Aeronautics and Space Administration) opened the Lyndon B. Johnson Space Center. The center provides astronaut training and is Mission Control for all space flights.

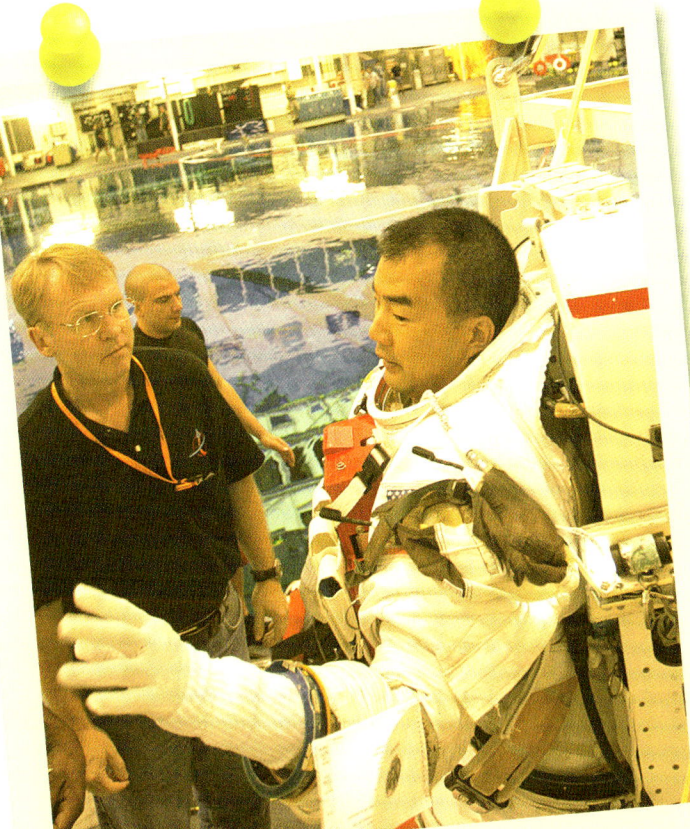

Astronauts Andy Thomas (left) and Soichi Noguchi test a space suit in a lab at the Johnson Space Center.

Life changed for Texans after the war, especially for African Americans and Hispanics. Since the end of the Civil War (1861–1865), these groups had faced **racism** and **segregation**. They were not allowed to use the same facilities as white citizens. Often, they were not allowed to vote. Many were the victims of violence. But in the 1960s, attitudes began to change. The **Civil Rights** movement slowly brought rights to all Texans.

Texas is not **immune** to the problems of society, but Texans remain proud of their state. Almost without fail, buildings that fly a United States flag will fly a Texas flag beside it. Texans take pride in the symbols of their state's history: the Alamo, cowboys, the Texas longhorn, oil **derricks**, and the Lone Star flag.

Texas Politics

During the 20th and 21st centuries, many Texas politicians gained national fame.

Lyndon B. Johnson, born in 1908 near Stonewall, became president of the United States in 1963.

Barbara Jordan, born in 1936 in Houston, was the first African-American congresswoman to come from the Deep South. She was also the first African American to deliver a **keynote speech** at a **political convention**.

Texas is also the home of one of only two sets of father-and-son presidents. George Herbert Walker Bush became president of the United States in 1989. His son, George W. Bush, became president in 2001 and was re-elected to a second term in 2004.

43

Map of Texas

Timeline

9000 BCE	Paleo-Indians live in the Panhandle.
6000 BCE	People of the Archaic Period live on the Rio Grande.
700 CE	Caddo people live in East Texas.
1519	Alonso Álvarez de Pineda maps the Texas coast.
1528	The Álvar Núñez Cabeza de Vaca and Narváez **expedition** is shipwrecked at Galveston.
1541	Francisco de Coronado crosses the Llano Estadado.
1542	Remnants of Hernando de Soto's expedition enter East Texas.
1682	Tigua Indians build **Mission** Ysleta del Sur near El Paso.
1685	René-Robert Cavalier, Sieur de La Salle, builds a settlement near Lavaca Bay.
1690	First Spanish mission established in East Texas.
1713	Mission San Antonio de Valera is built at San Antonio.
1821	Texas becomes a Mexican state after Mexico breaks away from Spain.
1836	The Texas Revolution takes place; Texas becomes an independent republic.
1845	Texas ratifies a constitution and becomes the 28th state in the Union.
1846–1848	War with Mexico takes place.
1850	The Compromise of 1850 sets current Texas borders.
1861–1865	Texas joins the **Confederate** States of America; the Civil War takes place.
1870	Texas is readmitted to the Union.
1876	The current Texas constitution is adopted.
1881	The second continental railroad runs through Texas.
1888	The Texas capitol is completed.
1900	Six thousand people die in the Galveston hurricane.
1901	Spindletop oil well is established.
1958	Texas Instruments develops the first silicon chip.
1963	President John F. Kennedy is killed in Dallas.
1964	The Lyndon B. Johnson Space Center opens in Houston.
1976	Barbara Jordan is the first African American to deliver a **keynote speech** at a Democratic convention.
1988	George H. W. Bush is elected president of the United States.
1994	George W. Bush is elected governor of Texas.
2001	George W. Bush becomes president of the United States.
2004	George W. Bush is reelected to a second term as president of the U.S.
2006	Texas's **Gross Domestic Product (GDP)** exceeds one trillion dollars.

Glossary

Anglo American settler of English, Irish, or Scots descent

annex to add or invade

archaeologist scientist who studies civilizations from earlier times

architect person who designs and builds things

artifact object made by humans in the past that teaches us about them

blaze to cut through or mark, as with a new trail

brand mark on an animal that shows whom it belongs to

budget government's plan for using money

cat's-eye type of gemstone

cavalry soldiers on horseback

Christianity religion whose followers believe Jesus Christ is the son of God

civil rights citizens' basic rights, such as the right to vote

Confederate relating to the South during the Civil War

conquistador Spanish explorer and conqueror

conspire to join in a secret agreement to do something unlawful

constitution written laws of a country

crisis unstable state of affairs

culture beliefs, art, music, and history shared by a group of people

delegate person who represents others in political meetings

delirious mentally confused

derrick tower, over a deep hole dug to access oil, from which a drill can be supported

diamond stud button set with diamonds

empresario leader given authority by Mexico to bring settlers to Texas

Emancipation Proclamation document issued by Abraham Lincoln that freed some slaves in the United States

execute to put to death

exhibition public display of art or new machines

expedition journey made by a group of people

export to ship goods to another country to sell

Great Depression time from about 1929 to 1940 when many people lost their jobs and life savings

Gross Domestic Product (GDP) total value of the goods and services produced in one year

grievance cause of a complaint

immigrant person who moves from his or her country to live in another country

immune unaffected by a disease or problem

impeach to bring a charge against a public official

Indian Territory area, most of Oklahoma, set aside for Native Americans after they had been forced to leave their original homes

interim temporary

keynote speech speech, given to a political group, which outlines their key goals

Ku Klux Klan group of mainly white Christians who used intimidation and violence against those they did not agree with, mainly African Americans, in order to keep them from power

magnate powerful businessperson

mission building built for use by people (missionaries) who wish to convert Native Americans to Christianity

plantation large farm often run with help of slave labor

pneumonia illness of the lungs

political convention meeting of a political party to choose delegates

pueblo Native American village of connected houses

quarantine separation of people or animals from other people or animals to ensure diseases do not spread

racism belief that members of some races are inferior to members of other races

Red River Wars series of uprisings in 1874 and 1875 by Native Americans who had been forced to live on reservations

replica faithful copy of an original

reservation land set aside for Native Americans by the government

restore to make something as it was when new

salt dome land formation that contains salt deposits

secede to cut ties to the country to which one has belonged

Secretary of State person who acts on behalf of the president on matters between the president and foreign governments

segregation separation of groups of people based on race, religion, or culture

siege long attack on a place with the desire to conquer it

skirmish short battle, usually with few casualties

stampede wild rush of animals

subdue to put down

Tejano Texan of Mexican descent

title official paper stating that a person owns something, such as land

Union relating to the North during the Civil War

unique unlike anything or anyone else

Zuñi Native American people from New Mexico

Find Out More

Further Reading

Haley, James. *Stephen Austin and the Founding of Texas*. New York: Rosen Publishing, 2003.

Roberts, Russell. *Texas Joins the United States*. Hockessin, DE: Mitchell Lane Publishers, Inc., 2007.

Sievert, Terri. *Texas*. Mankato, MN: Compass, 2003.

Torres, John Albert. *The Texas Fight for Independence from the Alamo to San Jacinto*. Berkeley Heights, NJ: Enslow Publishers, 2006.

Website

http://www.texasbeyondhistory.net/
This site, from the University of Texas at Austin, provides fun and fascinating facts about Texas's cultural heritage.

Index

aircraft manufacturing 42
Alamo 9, 15, 16, 19
Archaic Indians 4
Austin, Moses 11
Austin, Stephen Fuller 11, 12, 21

Battle of San Jacinto 19
bison 4, 32
Borden, Gail 18
Bowie, James 14, 15
Buffalo Bayou, Brazos and Colorado Railway Company 34
Buffalo Soldiers 29
Burnet, David 17, 20, 22
Bush, George Herbert Walker 43
Bush, George Walker 43

Cabeza de Vaca, Álvar Núñez 5, 7
Caddo Indians 5
cattle business 33, 34–38
Centennial 42
Chisholm, Jesse 35
Chisholm Trail 35, 37
Cíbola (Seven Cities of Gold) 6, 7
Civil Rights movement 43
Civil War 27–31
Civilian Conservation Corps (CCC) 42
Clark, Edward 27
Compromise of 1850 26
Confederate States of America 27
conquistadors 5, 6, 7
constitution 12, 30
Coronado, Francisco de 6, 7
Cos, Martin Perfecto de 14, 18
cowboys 36, 37
cowgirls 37

Declaration of Independence (Texas) 15, 16, 18
DeWitt, Green 13
DeWitt, Sara Seely 13
Dickinson, Almaron 15
Dickinson, Angelina 15
Dickinson, Susanna 15, 17
Dorantes de Carranza, Andrés 7

Eberly, Angelina 23
Emancipation Proclamation 28
empresario system 11–12
Esparza, Gregorio 16
Espíritu Santo mission 9
Estevanico 7

Fannin, James Walker, Jr. 17
Ferguson, James 41
Ferguson, Miriam A. 41
Ford, John "Rip" 28
Fort Mason 27
Fort St. Louis 8
forts 8, 26–27
France 8–9, 10
Freedmen's Bureau 29–30

Garza De León, Doña Patricia de la 12
Gladys City Company 40
Glidden, Joseph R. 38
Goodnight, Charles 36
Goodnight-Loving Trail 36
Granger, Gordon 28
Great Depression 41

Higgins, Patillo 40
Houston Post 18
Houston, Sam 14, 17–20, 21–23, 28
hurricanes 40

immigrants 25, 26

Johnson, Lyndon B. 43
Joiner, Marion "Dad" 40
Jones, Anson 20, 22, 24
Juneteenth 28

Karankawa Indians 8

La Bahia mission 9
La Salle, René-Robert Cavelier, Sieur de 8
Lamar, Mirabeau B. 19, 20, 22
Lee, Robert E. 27
León, Martin De 12
Lincoln, Abraham 28
longhorn cattle 34–38
Loving, Oliver 36
Lyndon B. Johnson Space Center 42

Maldonado, Alonso del Castillo 7
Mexican War 25
Mission San Antonio de Valero 9
missions 7, 9, 10

Narváez, Pánfilo de 5
Native Americans 4–8, 12, 21, 22, 23, 26, 28, 31–32

oil 38, 39, 40–42
Old Blue (steer) 36

Paleo-Indians 4
plantations 27, 33
Polk, James K. 24, 25

racism 43
railroads 32–36
Reconstruction 29, 30
Red River Wars 32
Republic of Texas 20–24
Rio Grande 20, 25, 26

San Felipe de Austin 11
Santa Anna, Antonio López de 14, 15, 18–20
Saracen (stallion) 18
segregation 43
Seguín, Juan 19
settlers 11, 12
sharecroppers 30
Sherman, William T. 31–32
slavery 12, 27–30
Spain 5–8, 9, 10
state constitution 12, 24, 30
statehood 24

Tejanos 19
Telegraph and Texas Register 18
Texas Declaration of Independence 15, 16, 18
Texas Revolution 13–19
Travis, William 14, 15, 16
Treaty of Guadalupe Hidalgo 25–26
Treaty of Velasco 20
Twin Sisters (cannons) 17, 19

Victoria (town) 12

Washington-on-the-Brazos 12, 15, 16
Western Trail 36
Williams, Elizabeth "Lizzie" Ellen Johnson 37
Williams, Hezekiah 37
World War II 42–43

Zavala y Sáenz, Manuel Lorenzo Justiniano de 17, 20, 23